The Way She Blooms

A Poetry Collection

grace gegenheimer

ISBN: 978-0-578-68429-1

TO THOSE I LOVE

My sweet Casey—
for your unwavering love, patience and encouragement as I pursue
my dreams. you are the best husband and life partner one could imagine.

Claire—
my wise, resilient and strong little sister,
for teaching me to look at things differently.

Dad—
for putting the world right at my fingertips.

Mom—
for always letting me stay up just a little bit longer to read.

Janet—
for the tough love when I have doubts, and for giving me my first
Jane Austen book when I was 10 years old.

Carol—
for the adventures and conversations that inspired so many of these words.

My grandparents—
for being my strength and inspiration from above.

And to that voice in my heart—
thank you for not letting me stay silent.

I want to be so
immersed in this life
that when I descend
back to the earth,
poetry comes
pouring off of me
like rainwater.

CONTENTS

acknowledgments i

1 tiny words of wisdom (for the seekers) 1

2 that feeling of solace (for the dreamers) 47

3 stories and fairytales (for the believers) 69

4 the way she blooms (for all of us) 87

ACKNOWLEDGMENTS

I am going to be selfish for a moment—my heart and soul are in this poetry collection, and I have had to overcome my biggest obstacle (myself) to make it a reality. What you are about to read is the joy, the sorrow, the musings and the ramblings of a desert poetess with her head in the clouds. Take care of these poems… I have been through a lot with them.

I would like to thank the artist who so beautifully illustrated the cover—a Greek goddess by the name of Melpomeni Chatzipanagiotou. Thank you for dreaming up such lovely images and for your patience as we worked together from halfway across the world.

Thank you to my friend Alyssa Robinson for scattering your beautiful drawings across these pages. The way they dance with my words is lovelier than I could have imagined.

Thank you to Susan Nunn for keeping me focused and pushing me through the final stretch. I appreciate your words of encouragement, your guidance, and your support in navigating the publishing process.

Lastly, I would like to thank *you* for reading and being a part of this journey. I hope you see a bit of yourself in these poems.

– grace

tiny words of wisdom

Nostalgia can be bitter
or it can be sweet,
but it doesn't really matter
because I've always liked
the taste of memories.

The man on the moon
keeps me wondering
and waiting, but the
goddess I know as
Mother Earth stops
him in his tracks and
says to me

> "you only get to do this
> once – go out there and
> see what's been calling
> your name."

every one of us is trying
to make sense of this world,
and that is what keeps us wild—
hunting for answers and
searching for wisdom.
preying on truth
and feasting on knowledge.
clawing at ideas and
sinking teeth into dreams.
exploring the unknown
and chasing the wonders
of time.
wild we are, and wild
we will always be.

Hello little seedling,
you may not feel like much
right now, but believe me when
I say your existence is important.
One day you will know just
how much you are appreciated—
how much you are needed.
You will become something
tall and mighty, and able to
withstand any storm.
Until that day, little seedling,
keep growing. Keep reaching
for the sun. The promise of
another day is on the horizon,
and it's yours if you're willing
to reach for it.

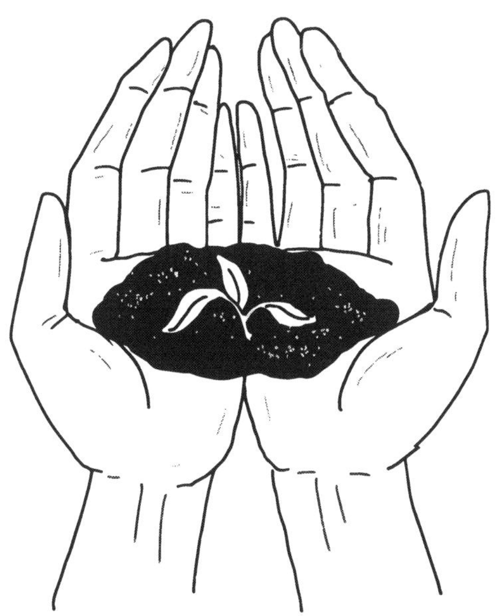

Take that storm by the hand—
unafraid, and ready for rain.

Be bold when you tell the mountains
that you will conquer them one day.

Now go find that staircase
that takes you to the sky,
and dance among the moonbeams
like the dreamcatcher you are.

Everyone has that one place
that just feels like childhood—
a place where nostalgia settles
into your bones as you are taken
back to another time.
And that gentle ache in your heart?
That is the undeniable longing for
simpler days when you lived
without a care in the world.
It hurts, doesn't it?
But still, you can't help but smile.

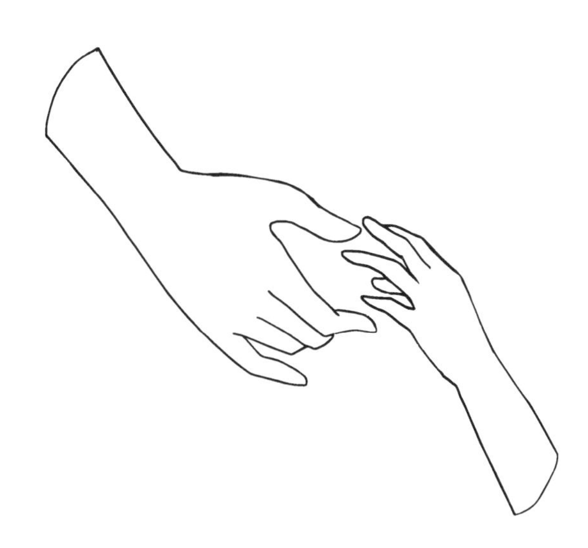

The human soul
(much like stained glass)
is a mosaic
of broken pieces
that still finds a way
to shine with
every touch of light.

You have shown
your beautiful and
sensitive heart to
the world,
and that is why
you hurt so much.

The moon sees us
exactly for who we are.
Tiny, vulnerable.
Lost, confused.
Perfectly imperfect—
and absolutely capable
of reaching the very stars
that surround her.

I know you're hurting
and you're tired
and you're losing hope—
but if you hold on
and ride that storm
into tomorrow,
you just might find the
other side of the rainbow.

Keep your inner child alive—
for to be a child is to be simply
and purely human.
Please tell me you have not
forgotten what this feels like.

Maybe your star just wasn't meant
to be part of my constellation.

I need you to stop
and look in the mirror.

You are a reflection
of every single person
who led to your creation,
and they are all alive
in this very moment
because there is breath
in your lungs
and blood in your veins.
You are living history,
a work of art,
a testament to the survival
of the human race.

Now, look at me
and tell me again
why you think
you are not important.

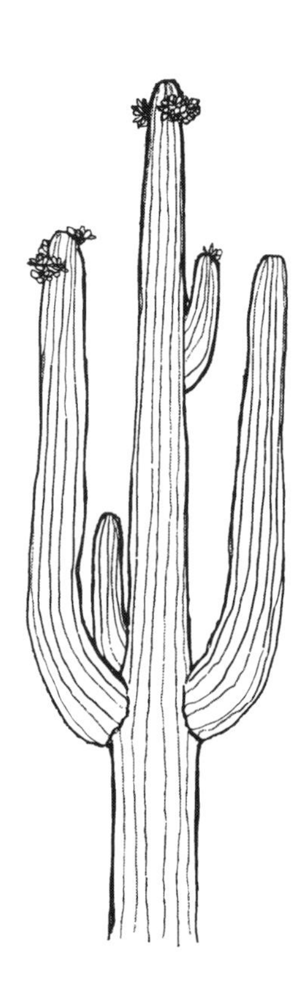

How many sunsets must you
chase to the edge of the sea
before you realize that the
moon is there to love you, too?

To forgive—
no matter
how much
it hurts,
is to have a
heart that is
capable of
the purest
form of
unconditional
love.

Start recognizing
and believing in
your own beauty.
There will never
be another you.

The bravest thing you
will ever do is keep
moving forward when
it feels like everything
is crumbling beneath
your feet.

She knows very well who she belongs to.

Herself.

The thing about poets
is we need heartache
and madness and loss
like the air we breathe—
for without the chaos,
words are just tiny
letters without a soul.

Every one of us is fragile.
So unbelievably fragile.
And the problem is that
we keep treating one another
as if our skin is made of
titanium and our bones are
sculpted from diamonds.
The reality is that we are
far more delicate than this.
Please—be careful with each other.

We are all just
curious little humans
with dreams in our
hearts and stardust
in our souls.

"It hurts. Why does everything hurt?"

"Because you love so big and most of them care so little."

you are enough.
you deserve love.
you matter.

where did we go so
wrong as a society
that we now have to
constantly remind
each other of such
simple things?

Don’t ever deny yourself the
freedom to feel beautiful.

So many people are already
going to try to take that from you.

When you
think about it,
"woman"
is just another
word for
resilient.

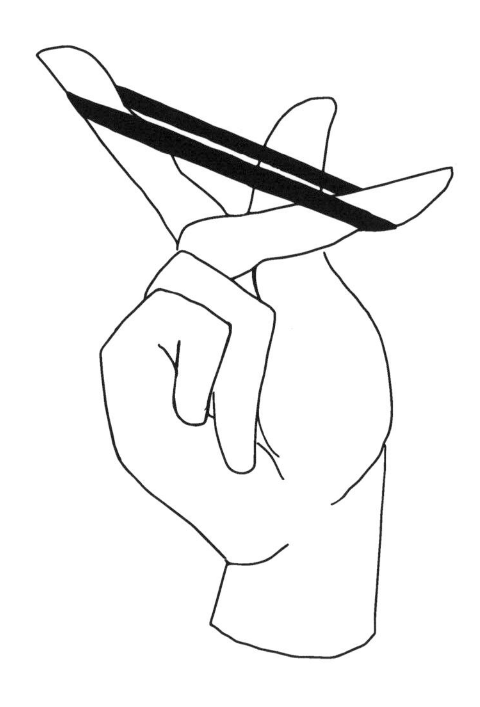

Like a tree in the forest,
it is important to stay
grounded in a world
that will constantly try
to uproot you.

All journeys on earth
must come to an end,
but if you look around
you will see that life is
written on every drop
of rain, every twisted
tree branch, and in the
melodies of the sea.
And in the midst of it all
you will realize that life
itself—by its very nature,
is truly never-ending.

Oh woman—
when will you see
that there is strength
in your sensitivity,
bravery in your tears,
and a world of words
behind that quiet smile?

You are beginning to
discover what the
mountains already know—
that you can move them.

Take care of those wings,
those precious wings—
for someday they'll take
you on a journey greater
than life.
I know right now is too
soon, but someday you'll
touch the moon.

- *a mama bird to her baby*

When you breathe in deeply,
you take in with you a piece of
all that exists in this world—
only to send it right back to
where it came from.

You are much more connected
to the universe than you realize.

Like the sun waiting to kiss the dawn,
you must learn to let patience prevail.

take emotion and truth,
put them on paper,
and give them a heartbeat.

that is poetry.

your soul
was meant
to be wild
and your
heart was
meant to
be free.

always
remember
this.

It's okay to write love letters to yourself—
and maybe you should from time to time.

sit quietly,
and really learn
the songs of
your heart.

hum along to
the melodies
that flow from
within and let
them evolve
into sacred
hymns that
guide your soul—

because you are
something of the divine.

But in the end, you have to be the
creator of your own wonderland.

To live,

    to truly live—

is not for the

faint of heart.

You talk of storms as if
they are a bad thing.
But my dear, they are
simply a time of trial,
and ultimately of triumph—
because they *will* pass and
you *will* survive.

I promise.

You must learn to put
your faith in the sun and
trust that it will help you
bloom into something
that even the moon
would be jealous of.

To be a woman is to
harness the power of
the earth below you,
sky above you, and
fire within you.

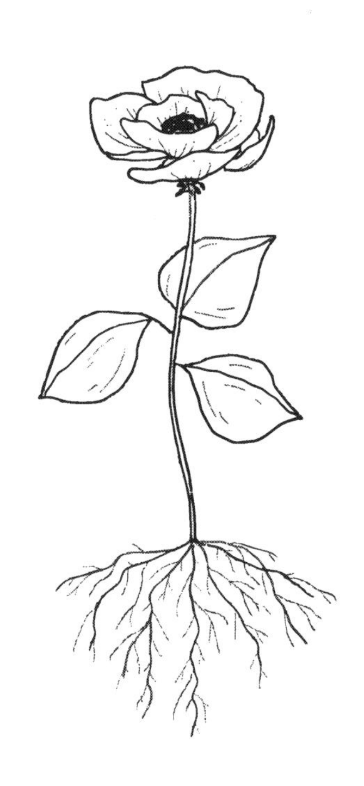

When you don't know
where to go but you
feel the winds begin
to change, be brave
and let them carry you.
Let them carry you.

You are powerful—
don't you know that?

You are beautiful—
can't you see that?

You are a child of the
heavens who has been
granted a short walk on
this earthly trail, and one
day you will return to the
stars where it all began.
So in these few fleeting
moments known as life,
trust your power,
acknowledge your beauty,
and know that your spirit
is right where it needs to be.

that warm feeling deep inside your chest?

  that is your soul on fire.

you must never let it burn out.

that feeling of solace

Oftentimes when she felt lost,
she looked to her ancestors.
She retraced their steps in her head
until her own path became clear.
It makes perfect sense, doesn't it?
After all, they are the ones
who brought her to this moment
and are the reason she stands
so bravely as she looks to the future.

Do not mind me if I talk to the moon—
for she understands me like no one else.
One day my soul will return to her,
and a glorious day that shall be.

The mountains whisper my name,
the forest beckons me to dance,
and the desert sings to me
the songs of my childhood.

But my eyes are always looking upward—
to a place I have never known.

The sky is everything to me.
It tells me all I need to know
and has given me strength
at times when earthly things
are too much to bear.

The echo of thunder makes me
want to run towards the storm—
for it reminds me of the way my
heart sounds when something
remarkable is about to happen.

The Moon and
the Earth are
bound in an
endless waltz,
and one day
they will hold
each other again.
But for now
they dance the
days and nights
and years away—
just waiting for
the music to end.

Just when I thought
I had forgotten how
to breathe underwater,
I hear a whisper from
the depths of the sea—
the heart of the ocean
reaching for my hand
and saying 'come find me.'

And so I step away from
the shore and return to
a place I knew long ago,
collecting pebbles and
fragments of memories
along the way.

The night itself keeps me awake.
It says "stay a little longer and
you will see that the mysteries
of the stars are also the
mysteries of the heart."

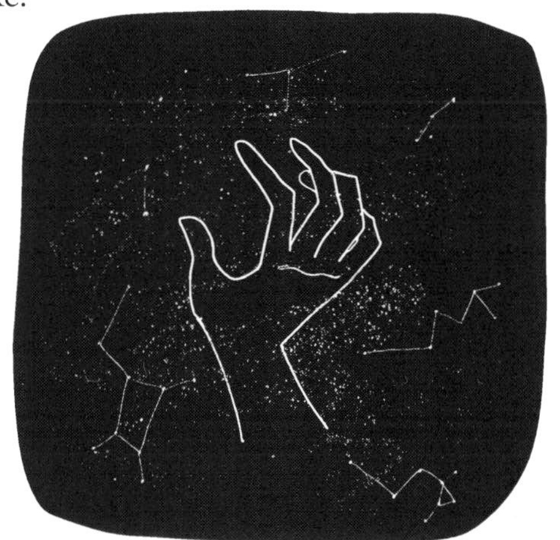

The moon then reveals
herself from behind the
clouds, and smiling down
at the world she says to me

"stay awake, my dear, and
you will find yourself when
you spend enough time with
a glitter-studded sky."

The miracle I see
reflected in the water
is a soul with my name—
and she is the
ocean's daughter.

darling girl,
you carry within you
a love for this world
that is so rare to find.
you smile at the sound
of rain. you close your
eyes and raise your arms
to the sun. you stop to
admire every tree and
every stone along your
way. believe me when I
say you are not like the
others. you hold the
entire universe in your
heart, and it shows. my
goodness, does it show.

Where I saw fragments,
you saw a mosaic—
and slowly you put the
pieces of me back together
until I resembled something
that could be considered art.

You have given
me a home in
your heart,
and you reside
just as much in
mine.

One day your heart will be
aching with sorrow and
uncertainty, and you will
hold the moon in your eyes
with the hope that it will
take you somewhere better.

And one day you will look at
the very same moon and say
"you held me safe under
your light when I thought
my world was going to end…
thank you."

ink may not last forever,
but words are eternal.
they are carried by the
winds of time,
transcending each of
our lives and all earthly
things.
so when you say that
all of us die someday—
i will remind you that
you were loved by a poet,
and a poet won't let you
fade into history like the
rest of them.

us humans have this intrinsic
fascination with the sky.
deep down, we all know there
is something wonderful that
lies beyond, and that we have
been there before and will
someday return to it.

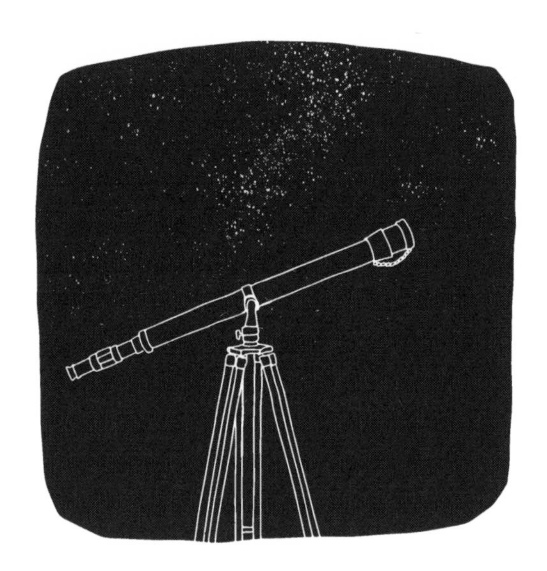

Like an ancient star
falling from the sky,
I find myself fading
gracefully into the
stillness of night.

- *sleep*

Remnants of flame
leap into the night,
and through the
embers of what
was once a mighty
elm tree—
I swear I can
almost see your
name.

I'd love to stay awake and pretend
to care about these earthly things…
but my heart belongs to the night
and I have a date with the stars.

The gospel of my soul
sounds a bit like the
gently falling rain
in wintertime.
The hymns of
my heart—
they sing along to
the clouds drifting by,
and it sounds an awful
lot like wind chimes on
a lazy Sunday afternoon.

well darling,
the stars are
a lot like love.
mysterious,
gentle and soft,
but burning so
brightly against
the darkness
of night.
and yes,
sometimes
they fall—
but they're
beautiful
while they shine,
aren't they?

stories
and
fairytales

The love affair
between my soul
and the universe
is quite the fairytale.

The Way She Blooms

The world is much too inviting
when you teach hummingbirds to sing,
and they call her name
as winter surrenders to spring.

And far beyond the rose garden
a ship sails past the northern star,
and it calls her name
to a rainstorm of paper hearts.

The safety of these castle walls
is perhaps a little too safe
for the queen with the flower crown
and the constellations in her eyes.

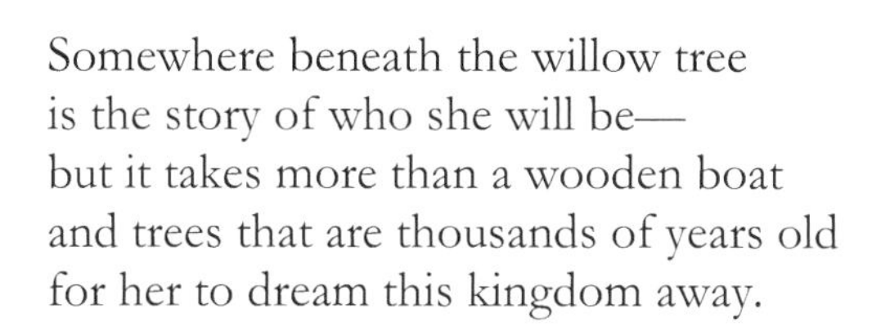

Somewhere beneath the willow tree
is the story of who she will be—
but it takes more than a wooden boat
and trees that are thousands of years old
for her to dream this kingdom away.

The world is much too inviting
when you teach fireflies to shine,
and they call her name
as sunlight whispers through the vines.

The thunder is but an old friend
when your heart belongs to the skies,
and it calls her name
waiting for the full moon to rise.

The queen with the flower crown
and the constellations in her eyes—
she walks barefoot towards the storm
as she leaves this kingdom behind.

It is a weary old world,
my dear,
and there are times
I feel I have lived too long.

These streets are empty now,
but they sure knew how to shine.
You should have seen this town,
sweet child,
during the days of my dancing feet.

It has been a hard life,
you know—
but we had music
and we had books,
and we always had the sun.

And come to think of it—
my childhood was sweet.
Such fond memories I have
of much simpler days,
when it was just me and my dancing feet.

I never thought I would grow old,
but my mother told me
it would happen to us all,
and I never believed her.
Boy did eighty years go by fast…

I would love to stay and tell stories,
my dear,
but the sun is shining
and I must go inside,
for I much prefer the rain these days.

- *the old jazz dancer from New Orleans*

In a place where words are given life—
that is where you will find me;
look no further than the heavens,
and no closer than the sea.

The path of a poet
is like shadows of the night,
where truth is whispered in the dark
but never sees the morning light.

The colors that flow from the earth—
they will find their way to my soul,
and like a winter sunset
this road will take me back home.

You cannot see it,
and you will not find it—
for this place that I speak of
has no beginning and no end.

The path of a poet
is curiously misleading—
it is some fantasy world
where even the stars are dreaming.

She came to me in a dream—
a woman of about eighty-five.
She must have seen the confusion
written in my eyes, for she sat
me down across from her
and asked what was wrong.

"I feel so lost."

"That's not always a bad thing, my dear."

I sighed. "It would just be nice to know
know where I'm going."

She smiled wisely, held my face in
the palm of her hands and said
"*Ah, but where's the adventure in that?*"

I find myself
being drawn to the trees—
and longing to become lost
in the forest.

I think I finally know why.
Is it because I wouldn't mind
being swallowed by the unknown?
Like Alice, I am curious
and perhaps brave enough
to follow the white rabbit.
I want to spend time
with the tulips,
and have tea with the ones
they call mad.

But if the Queen of Hearts
comes looking for revenge,
I will stand my ground
and say to her
"I am the Queen of Diamonds,
and unlike hearts,
diamonds do not break easily."

The Cheshire Cat would be proud,
and maybe the caterpillar
would no longer question who I am.
He has become a butterfly,
and I have become a little more me.

"And by the way, Your Majesty—
it was I who painted the roses red."

I was sitting on a bench
one chilly September day
when an old woman next to me
caught me looking at the sky.
She turned to me and said
"I can tell you're a dreamer, kid"
and smiled at me knowingly.

"I thought I had this world figured out,
and someday you will think the same.
But with every full moon,
and every summer night,
and every snowflake that falls,
I can honestly tell you—
I am still so amazed by it all."

We sat quietly for a while,
understanding each other's silence.
The gray clouds were familiar
but there was something strange
about this windy autumn day—
for somehow I already knew *her*
from a place I had been long ago.

Soon the breeze was calling her elsewhere
but before she got up to leave,
I glanced over at her, and saw *me*.
For in that magical moment
when two dreamers cross paths,
it is like looking in a mirror
to see all that you are and will be.

With grace in her every step
the old woman turned back once more
to say goodbye without a word.
I recognized that look in her eyes—

that look of an ambitious dreamer
with the wistful smile of a muse
who is much too in love with the world.

Ocean,
I've heard stories about
your tranquility—
about your crystal blue
waters that reach longingly
for the shore and speak of
times when the human
heart was one with yours.
We belong to you.
Let us return to you.

Ocean,
I've heard stories of how
dangerous you are—
of your violent storms
that swallow entire ships
and of depths that no one
has ever seen. But my heart
beats to the rhythm of your
waves, and I am not afraid.
I belong to you.
Let me return to you.

I heard the sound of flutes
and the beating of drums
as I made my journey
across the desert's red sand.

Far in the distance
melodious chanting
rang out towards the heavens.
And then I saw her—
a Navajo elder
beautiful and ancient
much like the sacred ground
upon which she walked.

Hardly able to speak
I said to the woman
"I do not know where to go."

With eyes dark as midnight
she beckoned for me to bow,
and adorned my neck with turquoise.
"Ask the mountains," she said.
"They know the way,
and they know you."

I fell to my knees,
overcome with thirst.
I gazed up ahead—
blinded by the sun,
and cried to the skies
"Oh blessed mountains,
how do I return home?"

When I looked back down
I saw it, clear as day.
Water.
Water—flowing gently

and carving deep veins
into the rain-starved earth.
The Navajo woman
was nowhere to be found.

I could not decide
if I had met her before,
or if she existed at all.
But I followed the stream,
until it brought me back home—
and with every step
her words echoed back to me
ask the mountains,
ask the mountains,
ask the mountains.

Maybe it was a premonition
or perhaps a distant memory,
but I had a life among the stars—
a glorious time when I was free.

I keep trying to forget
but it is engraved in my soul,
that the celestial beings above
can shine just as bright as gold.

I have heard that I am stardust
which has fallen from the skies,
and this is all that I am—
a tiny bit of paradise.

My soul is like the heavens
ancient and full of mystery,
no one knows the extent of either
because nobody really knows me.

In a place where Earth disappears
and Orion cannot be seen,
there is a land of faith and hope
and this is where you will find me.

I read by the light of the moon
and have danced with the northern lights,
I have discovered too many secrets
to be afraid of the night.

The constellations inspire me
reminding me of places I know,
each one tells a divine story
of wonders from days long ago.

It could have been a premonition

or perhaps a distant memory,
but I dream of that life among the stars
as if it were still a part of me.

Nothing but debris and
last winter's leaves are
scattered on this old floor.
Shards of glass reflect the
barren trees above, where
one lonely crow still soars.

Lying face-down in the dirt
is a framed portrait of a child—
she must have been the one
who left behind her tiny red
leather shoe at the door.

Did they leave in pursuit of gold
just like the rest of them?
Or were they driven away
the first time they heard
this forest breathe?

These walls are now
crumbling and empty
except for the soft green
moss that resides in the cracks,
and in my amazement
the hauntingly beautiful
reality sets in—that when
we are gone, nature will slowly
take back what is hers.

grace gegenheimer

Sooner or later,
everyone comes 'round
the Poisoned Glen.
Gone are the days of
monsters and creatures
from land and sea,
but the legends remain—
and how could they
not be true?

Somewhere, trapped in
the fog is the still-beating
heart of these mountains—
and it echoes underneath
my feet.

I knew that one day
I would come 'round
the Poisoned Glen,
but I did not know
that it would already
be so familiar.
I did not know that
it would feel like home.

The winds were whispering
to her again—and this time
it sounded like adventure.
It was that same familiar
tune she had been waiting for.

the way
she
blooms

I carry within me
the heart of a warrior,
the mind of a pharaoh,
the soul of a goddess
and the wisdom of
my grandmothers'
grandmothers.

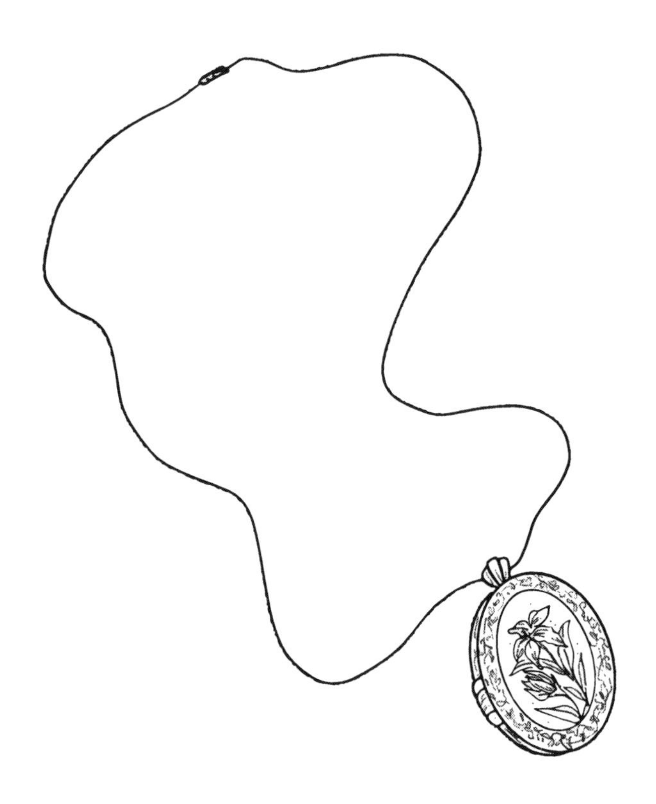

Sometimes I feel just like
the moon in that I have
seen too much.
But also like the moon,
it is my destiny to bring
light into a world that can
seem so dreadfully dark—
and so I have no choice.
I cannot turn away.

I'm treading through
troubled waters, but
not like the waters of
any river or ocean I
have been in before.
No—what I am seeing
is the perilous depths
of my own mind, and
the time has come for me
to decide if I sink or swim.

Through the mist I see a
light—a flicker of hope.
And when I reach that
light, my soul will finally
speak after a season of
heartache and pain.
It will say "there is nothing
in this universe that will ever
break me. I am a child of the
stars and one day my spirit
will rise higher than the tallest
mountains, just like it used to."

Until that day, I promise to keep
fighting. I promise to be patient
with me. I promise that I will
survive these troubled waters.

I open my heart to the skies
and it pours like a monsoon.

But I try opening it to others
and it is nothing but that
same desert drought.

I'm so sorry that I push
you away, but how else
will I find out if you're
going to stay?

People have hurt her,
and nature has saved her.
That is why there is such
gentleness in her voice
when she speaks about trees.

"What's wrong?" people ask me.
"Nothing" is my rehearsed reply.

But the truth is, my heart just hurts a little bit on most days. I look around and see wounds I cannot heal, people I cannot rescue, and a world I cannot save. I am constantly haunted by the thought that I am not doing nearly enough with this one tiny life I was given, and sometimes it is just too much for me to handle.

"No, nothing's wrong..."

The problem is—
there is absolutely
nobody in this world
who cares about me
more than I care
about them.

My heart outgrew
my rib cage long ago
and one day it will
destroy me.

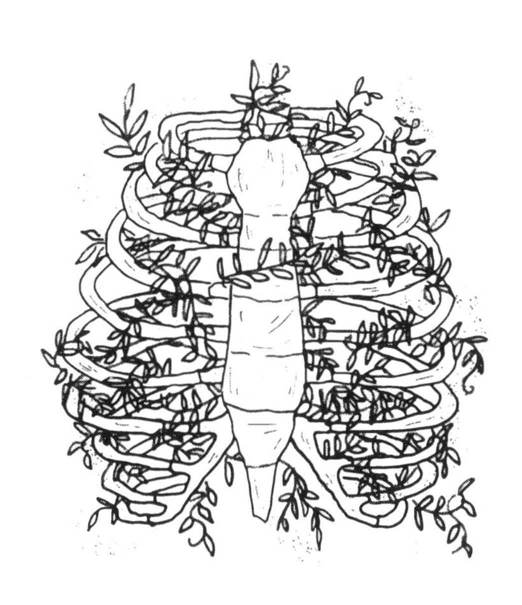

On some of my hardest days,
I listen closely until all I hear
are echoes from the past—
and one by one they whisper
to me

> "my love, your heart is
> so in the right place. You are
> ambitious and brave, and
> that brilliant mind of yours is
> overflowing with the stories
> of your ancestors. We are all
> so proud of the story you are
> writing for yourself. Do not
> be afraid of the future, for
> you will never walk into it
> alone. You have the wisdom
> of thousands of years
> forever at your side."

I promise you will find me, for I am not lost.
You will see me from where the daisies grow,
and I will gladly take you by the hand.
I have been wandering for far too long
and I think it's time to come home.

I write for the stars,
because I took a
part of them with me
when I fell from my
place of happiness
high above the clouds.

I write for the stars,
because they held
me safely when I
thought the rest
of my sky was falling.
I owe them my life,
but I give them my words.

Like the fire that fades
into soft embers,
I'll take my time.

Like the flowers that bloom
in the darkness of night,
I'll take my time.

Like the broken heart that
sings after a long, hard winter,
I'll take my time.

Like a sinner
waiting to be saved,
like the storm clouds
on the brink of rain;
like the breeze in the air
when summer is over,
like the changing leaves
that fall in October,
I'll take my time.

I'll take my time,
I'll take my time.

I feel something stirring
in my heart that I have not
felt in the longest time.

Is it faith? Is it inspiration?
Or is it simply the awareness
of my own heartbeat?

Whatever it may be, it is a
comfort to know that my
rib cage is not an empty chamber.
Something inside me still lives,
and maybe one day I will be okay.

As I grow older, all the things I tried to hide from
ridicule and judgment are beginning to resurface.
My laugh. My style. My passions and interests.
My quirks. My sensitivity and my emotions. But this
time I will not bury them or push them away.
I am reclaiming all of me and I'll never let her go.
I made a promise to that quiet but strong voice inside
my head that keeps telling me
"you must never lose yourself ever again."

Return me to the mountain and
let me feed off the light and the
air closest to heaven.
Return me to the ocean and
let me ponder the depths and
the mystery of creation.
Return me to myself and let me
remember the reason and the
purpose for my journey.

I'm beginning to realize
that I am not meant to
be understood by the
rest of the world…

and I'm okay with that.

There have been times
when my spirit has been
crushed by the force of
an avalanche,
but somehow I always
found a way to climb out.

Now I soar above snow-
capped mountains and
the view is amazing.

There was no dragon after all—
it existed only in her mind,
and once she realized it was
the only thing that stood
between her and her wild dreams,
that old stone tower collapsed
around her and the beast
was nowhere to be found.

Standing on the edge of the world,
I breathe to the rhythm of the ocean
with starlight reflected in my eyes.
It has been a while since I felt so small,
but also since I felt so brave.
I smile as I think to myself
“my spirit is very much untamed.”

I am resilient,
and I am stronger
than I appear.
Like the fire
I may burn out,
but like the phoenix
I shall rise from the ash.

I gotta tell you—
I'm really proud of
this heart of mine.

I was lost at sea—
surrounded by turbulent
waters that tried many
times to break my spirit
and keep me from
chasing after my dreams.

But nothing could stop me—
not even the ocean.

Now you will find me on the
other side of the rain clouds—
for I have become the storm
I always knew I was.

Cactus flowers grow and live so bravely.
They remind me that though the world
may be harsh and unforgiving, I can
choose to bloom in quiet strength,
just as they do.

I am not a tornado,
and not a hurricane.
I am not an earthquake
or an avalanche
or a monsoon.

I am a different
kind of storm—
a storm that is
simply called ***woman***.

And it is known
across all seven seas
that any storm
by that name
is the most powerful
force of nature to exist.

I am very much like Rome.
There is beauty to find among
my ruins, and at the heart of
me you will find the strength
of not only a warrior—
but of an entire empire.
I have been torn down
and rebuilt and I have
heard that I will stand
the greatest tests of time.
And one day, a young girl
will wander these streets
to listen to my stories of
defeat and triumph, and—
in all her bravery, she will
be inspired to build an
empire of her own.

If only you knew how wild and
whimsical and full of fairytales
this heart of mine is.

the river runs wild,
just as I do.
but unlike the river,
I will not run forever.

one day I will take
to the skies and
surround myself
with dreams and
rain clouds, but as
night falls and the
stars come to life,
I shall return safely
to the ground.

and to keep my
promise to that wild
river, I will come back
bearing a storm.

I tried staying still,
but something was
calling my name.

If they come looking, tell
them I ran away and found
my happiness in a meadow
of dreams and a field of
sunflower magic.

The mountains behind me
were born with the rest of the world,
but the age of my soul
is old as time itself.

I have lived a thousand truths
and my heart is full of ancient songs.
My mind resides in a place that was
forgotten long ago, but it is the
only place that makes sense
and feels like home.

And still, they look at me
with unknowing eyes and say
"*you're so young.*"

I cannot explain the magic
that happens when a poet
begins to see themselves as an
artist, and not just someone
who writes.

When my mind wanders,
it is usually caught somewhere
between a favorite memory and
daydreams that will never happen.

I very much
enjoy being lost
in my own world.
Reality doesn't
suit me.

The child within me
still watches butterflies
and wonders where they've been;
I hope the rest of their journey is
just as spectacular as
when it began.

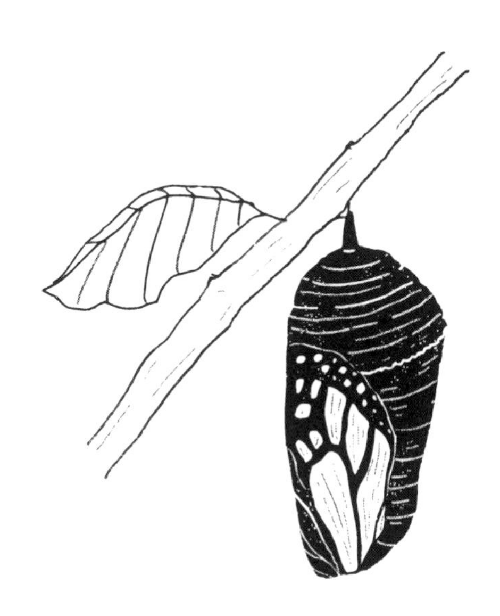

Part of me feels that home is right here at my feet—
but home is also that unreachable place that lies
beyond the stars and resembles neither a dream,
nor any reality I have lived in.

Here I stand between the two—marveling at the
heavens while gathering moonlight in my arms and
tossing flower petals into the wind.

And I realize for the first time that home is wherever
my heart feels free.

I dream in colors that are not
known to the rest of the world.

She was a goddess—
not because she was beautiful,
but because she carried the kind
of gentle love in her heart that
you only read about in fairytales.

God—
give me the strength to smile
at each and every storm,
and the courage to chase
the most relentless of them all.

I spent my entire childhood
looking up at the stars,
wondering if they shine
so beautifully just for me.

But after one cloudy, starless
night not too long ago, I realized
that it is *I* who shines for them.

You see, I am made of stardust—
and it radiates through my soul
and bursts through my fingertips
to illuminate the sky in a way
that no constellation ever could.

My spirit is not a candle,
but an eternal flame.

I shall never be extinguished.

I have learned to whisper my
dreams only to the wind, for
the heavens have always known
I am destined for something
much greater than myself.

A star cannot be a dandelion,
and a dandelion cannot be a star.
But regardless of their differences
I make wishes upon both, for I
would be a fool to deny that they
can both reach the heavens far
more easily than I—and I have
nothing to lose in putting my
faith in such simple magic.

You have a heart that still wants to
believe fairies sleep in hollowed-out trees.

You have a mind that dreams of braiding
flower crowns on warm summer days.

You open your arms to embrace the breeze—
letting it run through your fingertips and
into your soul.

You have hands that reach for the sun
and praise the rain.

You have a spirit that is wild and carefree,
yet grounded and strong.

Most importantly, you have a soul gentle
enough to remember things the rest of
the world has forgotten.

I have this feeling that I will always be in
search of something which has no name—
and may not even exist.

Let me be a muse.
Let me hear the
stories behind
timeless wisdom
that Socrates and
Plato and Aristotle
knew as truth.
Let me feel a
power within
that comes from
a being much
greater than us.
Tell me what the
ancient ones knew.
Let me be a muse.

Today I am
pursuing the
wild within
my soul,
and this time
they will not
be able to take
it from me—
for wild is all I
really am and
will ever be.

I almost forgot
what it feels like
to have a heartbeat
that runs along
with the wind…

your heart feels heavy—
but in the best kind of way.
it feels heavy because you
were born to feel that ache
of knowing there is
something out there much
greater than any of us.
you don't know what it is,
but you know it exists—
and this is what will drive
your sense of wonder
for the rest of your days.

I am not a rose
in a perfectly
manicured garden—
I am a wildflower
on rocky hillsides
and in meadows
that run alongside
snowmelt streams.
I will grow whether
you choose to care
for me or not,
because my
blooming is only
between me,
the rain and
the sun.

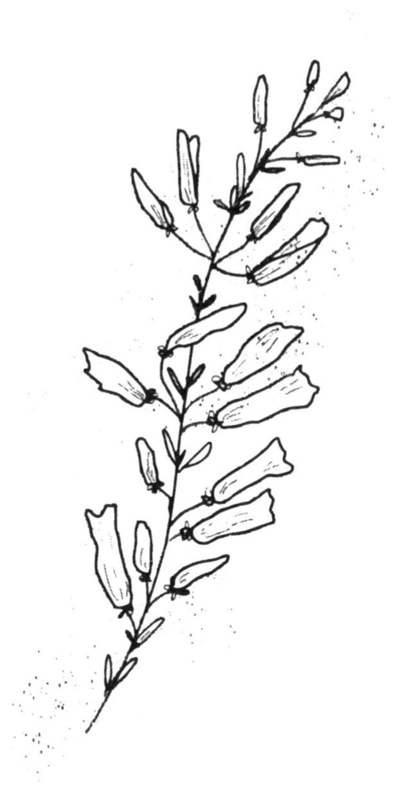

My soul is made of
crescent moons and
constellations,
of tiny promises and
childhood dreams.
My soul is made
of wildflowers
kissed by the
light of the sun's
golden hour.
It is made of the
stories I never heard,
and the words I will
never forget—

and I never forget.

To the mountains reaching for the sky, give me strength.

To the sunsets that fade into night, give me hope.

To the thunder that echoes in my soul, give me courage.

To the songs whispered by the sea, give me peace.

And to the stars reflected in my eyes, give me guidance.

Help me to find joy in this journey, and to know that I am never alone.

She is not to be tamed—
for like most goddesses,
she's got a fire in her belly
that gives her this hunger for life
and it will forever keep her wild.

All things good in this world
encircle her like feathers and
fairy dust, and she walks with
the strength of thousands
who journeyed before her.

She is not to be doubted—
for like most dreamers,
she's got a symphony in her soul
that sings the songs of the earth
and it will forever keep her grounded.

It is known that magic arises
from that quiet space where
your breath meets the wind—
but she is one of the few who
truly knows how to dance with
the breeze that whispers her name.

Courage gathers in her eyes
like storm clouds amid
soft evening skies.
Now watch what happens
when you step away and
give her some room—
she will laugh and she will cry
as she calls upon the sky to guide her

and that's just the way she blooms.

ABOUT THE AUTHOR

grace gegenheimer's poetry journey began at the tender age of seven when she received her first journal for christmas, and she hasn't put down her pen since. a self-described "daughter of the desert," grace is a ninth-generation native of tucson, arizona and is undeniably proud of her heritage. when she isn't writing, grace can often be found playing tourist in her hometown, hiking in her beloved catalina mountains, or boarding a plane to places near and far—always looking for inspiration and cool rocks to collect along the way.

Made in the USA
Middletown, DE
14 August 2020